Collected Short Lyric Pieces

for Solo Piano

By William Gillock

CONTENTS

ISBN 978-1-4803-4245-3

EXCLUSIVELY DISTRIBUTED BY

WILLIS MUSIC.

HAL•LEONARD®
CORPORATION
7777 W. BLUEMOUND RD. P.O. BOX 13819
MILWAUKEE, WISCONSIN 53213

Visit Hal Leonard Online at
www.halleonard.com

For Carolyn Jones Campbell
Drifting Clouds

William Gillock

From *Accent on Solos*, Level Three
Copyright 1969 by The Willis Music Co.

For Susan Alexander

Slumber Song

William Gillock

From *Piano - All the Way*, Level Four
Copyright 1969 by The Willis Music Co.

For Bea and Bill Carney

A Memory of Paris

William Gillock

With a lilt; in the French popular style

From *Seven Pieces in Seven Keys*
Copyright 1983 by The Willis Music Co.
Transposed and Revised 1993

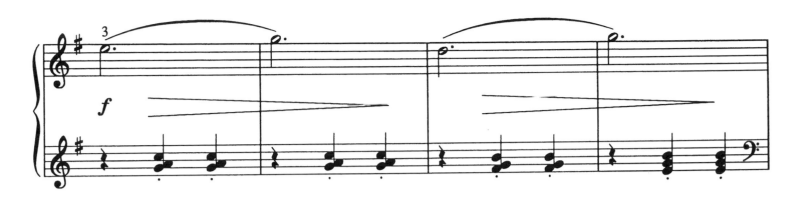

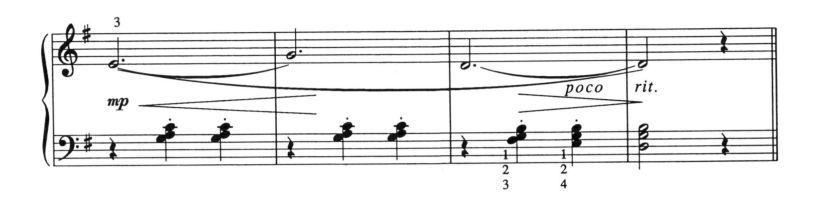

For Tate Yamashita
Mountain Ballad

William Gillock

For David Engle

Summer Clouds

William Gillock

With leisurely movement

* portato touch

From *Piano - All the Way*, Level Three
Copyright 1969 by The Willis Music Co.
(Original key G-flat major)

For Gloria Sanborn

Intermezzo

William Gillock

From *Piano - All the Way*, Level Four
Copyright 1969 by The Willis Music Co.

For Enid Wheeler

Petite Etude

William Gillock

From *Piano - All the Way*, Level Four
Copyright 1969 by The Willis Music Co.

For Karen Austin

Land of Pharaoh

William Gillock

With slow, sultry motion

Broadly; expansively

From *Accent on Majors and Minors*
Copyright 1963 by The Willis Music Co.
Transposed and revised 1993.

For Catherine Rollin
Homage to Chopin

William Gillock

For Glenda Austin

On the Champs-Élysées

With a steady dance beat and minimal rhythmic nuance

William Gillock

2nd time to ⊕

From *Accent on the Black Keys*
Copyright 1964 by The Willis Music Co.
(Original key D-flat major.)

D.C. al Coda

Coda

For Hiroko Yasuda

Postlude
(A Remembrance)

William Gillock